Page Turn

CW00350680

Oscar's Journey

Fiona Joseph

Series Editors:
Sue Leather and Rob Waring

NATIONAL
GEOGRAPHIC
LEARNING

CENGAGE
Learning·

Australia • Brazil • Japan • Korea • Mexico • Singapore • Spain • United Kingdom • United States

Page Turners Reading Library
Oscar's Journey
Fiona Joseph

Publisher: Andrew Robinson

Executive Editor: Sean Bermingham

Associate Development Editor:
Sarah Tan

Director of Global Marketing:
Ian Martin

Senior Content Project Manager:
Tan Jin Hock

Manufacturing Planner:
Mary Beth Hennebury

Assistant Editor: Jessie Chew

Layout Design and Illustrations:
Redbean Design Pte Ltd

Cover Illustration: Eric Foenander

Photo Credits:
98 Hemera/Thinkstock
99 Zoonar/Thinkstock
100 iStockphoto/Thinkstock
101 iStockphoto/Thinkstock

Library of Congress Control Number:
2012936337

ISBN-13: 978-1-4240-4893-9

ISBN-10: 1-4240-4893-1

National Geographic Learning
20 Channel Center Street
Boston, Massachusetts 02210
USA

Cengage Learning is a leading provider of
customized learning solutions with office
locations around the globe, including
Singapore, the United Kingdom, Australia,
Mexico, Brazil, and Japan. Locate your local
office at:
international.cengage.com/region

Cengage Learning products are represented
in Canada by Nelson Education, Ltd.

Visit National Geographic Learning online at
ngl.cengage.com

Visit our corporate website at
www.cengage.com

Printed in the United States of America
1 2 3 4 5 6 7 – 16 15 14 13 12

Contents

Review

Background Reading

People in the story

Oscar Keen
a 21-year-old man who
is meant to take over
Keen's Biscuits

Charles Keen
Oscar's father and owner of
Keen's Biscuits

Helena
Oscar's artist friend with
whom he is hoping to have a
relationship

Tom Harper
the foreman at Keen's
biscuit factory

Cecile Johnson
a young woman who lives on
the island of St. Christopher

Mr. Gaston
the owner of the sugar
plantation on St. Christopher

The story takes place in London and Birmingham in England, and
on St. Christopher (St. Kitts), an island in the Caribbean.

Chapter 1

Looking forward to a holiday

London, 1900

Oscar Keen was bent over his office desk, copying sales figures into the book. He tried to make his writing as neat as possible, knowing one single mistake would mean having to begin all over again. Mr. Allsop, his boss, was very strict about that.

He glanced up at the clock. Almost midday. And still twenty more receipts to copy. He dipped his pen into the ink bottle and tried to hurry. If only he could stop yawning.

Last night he'd gone to dinner with his friends as usual. At the start of the evening he promised himself he'd come back early and get a good night's sleep. But when he was with his friends—Helena, William, and Joel—his good intentions melted away like the ice cubes in his glass. Nine o'clock became ten o'clock, then eleven, midnight, as they talked and laughed long into the night. Then, before he knew it, morning had arrived and he was hurrying into his suit and racing across town to get to work.

Yesterday at dinner had been exciting though. Oscar and his friends had made the final plans for their trip to Switzerland. They were all taking their painting equipment. William, who was the most gifted artist of them all, took it very seriously. "You won't believe the sights in Switzerland . . . the snow on the Alps, the way the light catches on the mountains," he said. For Oscar, the holiday would also be a chance to get close to Helena, to find out how she really felt about him. For a long time he'd had an idea that she found him attractive, and he'd been pleased when Helena suggested that the two of them meet today to buy the travel tickets for the group.

Oscar sat back in his chair and ran his hands through his dark curly hair. One day they would all be famous artists. He could picture his paintings in a gallery next to Helena's work, with the critics crowding round in amazement and wealthy buyers asking him to do a painting for them. He imagined the pleasure of a lifetime devoted to his art and his friends.

Now look what you've done, said Oscar to himself, as he noticed ink all over his jacket sleeve. He really must concentrate and stop thinking about art and holidays and Helena.

It was no good, he decided. The bills and receipts would have to wait until he got back from meeting her. He stood and stretched his arms and shook his fingers to relieve their stiffness. Putting his jacket on quickly, he walked down the narrow stairs, trying not to make a noise so he could sneak past his boss's office on the ground floor.

He was almost there. He eased open the front door and then—"Oscar!" He heard Mr. Allsop's deep voice. "Would you come in here?"

He turned round slowly expecting to get a telling off, but instead Mr. Allsop's face was filled with anxiety and concern. His boss was holding out a letter. "Come and sit down, Oscar," Mr. Allsop said. His voice told him that it was not good news.

"It's your father," Mr. Allsop said.

"My father?" Oscar said in surprise. His father, Charles Keen, was the owner of Keen's Biscuits and he managed the factory in Birmingham over a hundred miles away. Charles had his own ideas for Oscar's career. Last year he had sent Oscar to London to work for his old friend, Mr. Allsop, so he could learn all about the world of business from a man who was a trusted business expert. Oscar had last seen his father a few months ago. Surely nothing could have happened to him.

"This news is not good, I'm afraid. Your father has been taken ill quite suddenly." Mr. Allsop put the letter down and walked around his desk to rest his hand on Oscar's shoulder. *So he's alive at least,* Oscar thought with relief.

"Of course," Mr. Allsop continued, "you must return to Birmingham immediately."

"But—"

"I can release you from your training. Go home right away, Oscar. Your father will need your help with the business until he recovers."

Feeling shocked, Oscar caught the train and arrived back at his boarding house.

Mrs. Douglas, who owned the house where he was staying, was surprised to see him. She helped him to pull down the large chest from the attic room. She began packing his clothes, carefully folding the smart white shirts he was obliged to wear to work—the hated shirts that he could never wait to tear off as soon as the office day ended and he could go out with his friends for the evening.

His friends! Helena! The holiday! He suddenly remembered he was supposed to be meeting Helena in the Square. Oscar opened the window and called out to a small boy playing in the street below. "You! I need you to go to the Square and take this message for me." He tore a page from his sketchbook, wrote a few lines to Helena, and then wrapped the note around a coin, which he threw to the boy. "Quickly. It's urgent!"

He was sure Helena would forgive him once he explained the situation. He could imagine the concern in her gentle green eyes as the news of his father's illness was passed on to her.

Mrs. Douglas had finished the packing. "Give my best regards to your father, Oscar. I hope he recovers quickly. You have been my worst house guest," she said, waving her finger at him. "Don't think I never heard you sneaking in during the small hours of the morning. But I shall be sad to see you go nevertheless. Come here, you bad boy." She gave him a hug. "Now sit on this chest for me and let's see if we can get it closed."

By the time Oscar arrived at the train station he was much calmer. Helena had got his message and the sight of her lean figure as she came running along the platform improved his spirits.

"Oscar!" she said. "Do you really have to leave? What about the holiday?"

How could he tell her how badly he wanted to go to Switzerland? How could he tell her that he secretly wished he'd left the office five minutes earlier and so missed the terrible news?

"I must go and see my father," Oscar said. "But you never know, he may not be so ill after all. Maybe I can still come on the trip. I could join you a little later." As Oscar spoke he thought, yes, why not? Perhaps he could hire a nurse for his father—someone who would do a much better job of caring for a sick man than he would anyway.

The whistle for the train blew. It was time to say good-bye. Helena took a card out of her bag. "Take this. This is where we'll be staying."

"Go," he said. "Tell William and Joel I'll come to Switzerland as soon as I can." He brought her hand to his lips and briefly kissed the material of her glove. "Just a few days," he said. "I promise."

On the train journey to Birmingham, Oscar looked at his reflection in the window, recalling how Helena had once called him a handsome fellow. He was tall, like his father, although much slimmer, and he had his mother's dark brown hair.

It was so unfair that his plans had been spoiled. Goodness knows, he deserved a holiday after working so hard in Mr. Allsop's office these past few months. Mr. Allsop was kind enough, and he meant well, but Oscar couldn't share his passion for business goods, or "commodities" as Mr. Allsop called them. Who in their right mind could get excited about the buying and selling of ordinary groceries like tea, coffee, and sugar?

Oscar was desperate for a different kind of excitement, one that was only satisfied when he was with his friends. Long evenings talking about art and literature and life with Helena, William, and Joel—now that was the real thing. The only problem was having to get up early for work the next day. Each time he dragged himself to the office, he felt like an animal being forced back into its cage. It hadn't been so wrong to want a holiday from all that, had it?

Now, as the train pulled into the station, Oscar wondered exactly what he'd find at home. Just how ill was his father?

Chapter 2

A son's return

They pulled up outside Oscar's family home. He paid the driver and Frank, his father's servant, came out. "Master Oscar. Thank goodness you've come." He helped the driver lift Oscar's heavy chest to the ground. "I'll deal with this. Go inside and see your father."

Oscar went through the open front door and was greeted by a row of other staff. This was home, as familiar to him as anything—the potted plants in the hallway, his father's collection of birds in their cages singing as if welcoming Oscar home.

"Where's my father?"

The cook replied, "Up in his room with the doctor. We had to call him out again this morning; your father was taken ill in the night."

Oscar walked up the stairs, his legs heavy as if they were filled with sand. His heart beat quickly and a sense of fear filled his stomach. Family paintings hung on the wall. Oscar stopped, as he always did, at the picture of his beautiful mother with himself when he was seven, shortly before she died. Touching her face, he remembered her final words to him, "Look after your father. He will need you when you're older." He carried on up the stairs.

A new picture of his father had been added to the collection. In this one he still appeared tall and

well-built with the familiar rosy cheeks that gave him a cheerful look. The artist had given his father a bit more hair than he possessed, but otherwise it was a convincing likeness. Charles Keen stood behind a table on which lay various packets of Keen's Biscuits. He had been painted to celebrate his forty-fifth birthday and the successful launch of their new line of cream biscuits. It was yet another accomplishment for Keen's Biscuit Company.

His father's door opened and a young man, whom Oscar guessed to be the doctor, came out.

"Are you the son?"

Oscar nodded. "Can I . . . ?"

"Go and see him? Well, alright, but only for a few minutes. He is very weak. Come and see me afterwards so we can discuss his health requirements."

Oscar walked into the room and shut the door softly behind him. His nose was filled with the smell of sickness. He approached his father's bed cautiously.

Charles Keen was sitting up, supported by cushions. His head rolled to one side as though his neck was not strong enough to hold it up. All the flesh had disappeared from under his cheeks. His skin was pale, with pink spots, and his breathing was noisy.

Oscar sat down on the edge of the bed and took his father's hand. It felt burning hot. Charles Keen had a fever.

"Father, it's me. Can you hear me?"

His father's head rolled the other way and his eyes stayed shut.

Outside the room the doctor was waiting.

"What exactly is wrong with him?" Oscar asked.

"Well," the doctor said, "I suspect it's influenza, but complications have set in. His heart is weak, and he needs complete bed rest for at least a month."

Oscar was called down to the dining room where Cook had prepared him his favorite beef dish and apple pie to follow. He ate the meal hungrily. When he had almost finished, Cook brought a note for him. "Tomorrow morning," it said, "Mr. Tom Harper, the supervisor at Keen's Biscuits, would be coming to the house to discuss some urgent business matters. Could Oscar be ready for a meeting at eight o'clock?"

Suddenly Oscar was hit by tiredness after the day's events. Only this morning he had been planning his holiday and now those plans had been turned upside down. There was nothing for it but to go to bed. He spooned the last of the apple pie into his mouth and stood up. "Time for bed, I think," he said, yawning. It was the first time in many months that he'd gone to bed before midnight.

Oscar went to sleep straight away but started to dream. He was climbing up a steep mountain path with Helena, breathing in the fresh woody scent that came from the nearby trees. Behind him, their friends William and Joel were arguing, jokingly, about who was the better artist. Oscar stopped walking and sat down for a while in the sun, feeling the most contented he'd ever been. He smiled across at Helena, who touched his arm and began speaking urgently to him. But the words didn't make sense. On and on she went, all the time shaking his arm, until the words finally made their way into his consciousness. "Master Oscar, you must wake up. Mr. Harper is downstairs waiting to see you."

Oscar woke with a start, wondered for a moment where he was, and then saw Cook leaning over him. He sighed and said crossly, "Alright, alright, you don't have to rush me."

He got dressed quickly and, before going downstairs, he paused outside his father's door, listening carefully until he could hear his father's breathing. Satisfied, but not wishing to go in, he continued downstairs. In the staff kitchen, he found a man of about fifty eating a piece of bread and butter spread with jam. The man stood up quickly and wiped his hands down his trousers.

"Why, you look familiar," Oscar said, "but I can't quite . . ."

"Tom Harper, sir. Foreman from your father's company."

"Foreman . . ."

"Yes, sir. I'm the one that makes sure that the production of the biscuits runs smoothly."

"Of course. Please sit down." He remembered that his father used to speak warmly of Tom Harper. Tom, Oscar knew, had worked at the factory since it opened twenty-five years ago. Clearly, Tom was now in a position of some authority at Keen's Biscuits. *Tom might just be the right man to help me,* Oscar thought.

"It must have been a shock for you to hear about your father," Tom said. He picked up his cap and rolled it around in his hands as he spoke. Oscar could see that he wanted to say something. "The thing is," Tom continued, "we were wondering what time you would be at the factory this morning. Tuesday is the day when we go over all the orders for the following week so we know how many boxes to produce."

Oscar was confused. What was the man talking about?

"What do you mean?" Surely they didn't expect him to go to the factory this morning?

"But sir, the thing is your father has put you in charge. He signed all the legal papers, sir. From now on, you are the boss of Keen's Biscuits. We can't do anything without your agreement."

Chapter 3

A visit to the factory

Oscar and Tom sat side by side in the carriage as the horse dashed down the lane and out of the grounds of the family estate. The morning sun cut through the trees, and Oscar was forced to close his eyes against the glare. His thoughts and feelings were all mixed up. Next to him, Tom made conversation but Oscar was barely listening. Events were moving out of his control.

Before leaving for the factory with Tom, he had gone up to see his father. There was no change in his condition. Charles lay on the bed, awake but still feverishly hot. "Father, can you hear me? We have to talk." But it was useless. All the words Charles muttered were pure nonsense.

Tom's voice broke into Oscar's thoughts. "Not far to the factory now. Do you remember coming here when you were a little boy? Your father used to let you sit on his desk, and the girls in the office would spoil you with treats when he wasn't looking." Tom appeared to be laughing to himself at the memory.

Oscar remembered little about the factory. After his mother died, his father sent him away to boarding school. Then, when Oscar turned twenty-one, his father told him he must go to London to begin his apprenticeship with his good friend Mr. Allsop. Oscar remembered him saying, "One day you'll take over Keen's Biscuits. And there's nowhere better than London

for you to receive your training. London is the center of the commercial world! Work hard, my boy, and in two years you'll return a man."

It looked as if that time had come, but much sooner than he expected. Don't worry, Oscar said to himself. He would go to the factory today, have a look around and then—with Tom's help—arrange for someone else to step in.

At the factory gates they stepped down and Tom took him into the building. They went past a reception area that looked dusty and untidy.

"Why is there no one at reception?" Oscar asked. Surely someone should be there to receive visitors and to take delivery of the post. Tom didn't answer. Perhaps he hadn't heard him.

Tom led Oscar to a door, on which there was a sign saying *Charles Keen, Managing Director*. Again, noted Oscar, the sign needed a polish. It didn't shine like the furniture in Mr. Allsop's office, where the front door shone so much you could almost see your reflection in it.

Tom opened the door and waved Oscar through it. His father's office was freezing cold. There was a fireplace, but it looked like a while since the fire had been lit and there was a smell of damp in the room. The desk was filled with papers and unopened letters. Oscar glanced at the pile but didn't want to touch it.

"What's been going on, Tom?" he said. "And why is there no one on reception?"

"Well, sir, I'm sorry to say things haven't been good for a while at the factory."

"What do you mean, not good?"

Tom stared at the floor.

"For goodness sake, Tom! Look at me and tell me what has been happening here."

"Your father hasn't been too well for quite a while. And, to be frank, the business has suffered as a result."

"You'll have to explain."

"Your father . . . well, he's become forgetful, mixing up orders and making other mistakes. He's upset some of the suppliers of our ingredients, trying to reduce what he'll pay for the raw materials, you know, flour and sugar . . ."

Oscar thought quickly. He was surprised. His father had always been strong and energetic and single-minded in his business goals. The picture that Tom was painting of his father was of a man who was too old and tired, a man who'd begun to make poor business decisions.

"But it's not just your father," Tom continued. "Times are changing. There's another company that started last year, a brand new biscuit manufacturer, and they seem determined to copy everything we do. Let me show you something."

Tom reached into Charles's desk and pulled out a packet of biscuits. Oscar recognized the box immediately. It was the lemon cream sandwich biscuits that Keen's had launched last year. He'd seen them in the shops all over London.

Tom gave the packet to him. "Look closely at the design of the box. Do you see anything unusual?"

"No. Should I?"

"Look again, sir," Tom said.

"Well, there's the green background, and the lemon tree, and the handwriting . . . Wait a minute, there's something different, something not quite right, but I can't put my finger on it."

Tom reached into the desk again and pulled out another packet. "Now compare it to this one."

Seeing the packets side by side it was easy to spot the difference. The tree on the first packet had four lemons, and on the second packet there were only three lemons. And how stupid he'd been! The first packet didn't say *Keen's Biscuits* at all. It said *Seal's Biscuits*. But someone had designed the letters to make the company names look almost the same. This was a very clever fake.

"Are you saying that this rival firm, this *Seal's*, is directly copying our designs? But how can that be? It's not legal, surely!"

"There's nothing we can do about it. The situation is even worse, I'm afraid," Tom continued. "Seal's are also selling their biscuits at a much cheaper price." He quoted a figure and Oscar said, "But that's 20 per cent lower than the price that my father has set."

"We can't compete with those prices. The thing is, sir," Tom said, "I heard a rumor that Seal's might be interested in making an offer to buy out Keen's. I tried to speak to your father about the idea but he wouldn't hear of it. He got very angry with me. What do you think? It could be the best option for Keen's Biscuits."

Oscar thought about this for a moment. He couldn't imagine his father ever agreeing to sell the factory.

But poor Tom had clearly been carrying a lot of the worry on his shoulders lately. Oscar tried to be positive for his sake. "So we have some competition? I'm sure once my father's better he'll have some splendid ideas for how to deal with this rival company." The words sounded false even to his own ears.

"Well sir, I'm glad you think so," said Tom. Oscar didn't like the way the supervisor said it.

Chapter 4

A challenge for Oscar

"Let me give you a tour of the factory," Tom said, slipping an overall on top of his clothes. He led Oscar past the unattended desk. "We had to release the receptionist earlier this year to save on costs. As well as one of the office clerks."

"We'll start with the mixing room." Tom directed Oscar into the room where two men stood on ladders that leaned against huge copper tubs. Oscar watched the men tip large bowls of flour and sugar and massive blocks of butter into the tub and then begin mixing the ingredients with an enormous wooden spoon.

Next door were the ovens for baking the biscuits. Here, the heat was intense and the workers' faces were hot and sticky with sweat. But the atmosphere seemed friendly and there was a great deal of laughter. Tom showed Oscar how the cooked biscuits were then put on wired sheets to cool, where they were stamped with the company's name before being delivered to the packing room. In this room the female employees worked on assembling boxes from sheets of card, and then another set of workers put the biscuits in the boxes. Oscar watched as a young girl expertly wrapped a ribbon around each box and the finished boxes were piled into huge wooden containers. "Once the containers are packed," Tom explained, "we carry them to the collection room next door for sending to our customers."

Oscar had observed that the workers were not fully occupied. "How many orders is my father getting every month?"

"You'll have to check the order book for the exact number but I can tell you that orders have been falling in recent months. And the costs of raw ingredients, especially the sugar, have gone up."

"Can you find your own way back to the office, sir?" Tom turned and began a conversation with one of the workers.

Oscar slipped away, glad to be left alone. He shut the office door, sat down in his father's chair and then lay his head on the desk. What on earth was he supposed to do next? To think only yesterday morning he'd been planning to meet Helena to buy their tickets for the trip to Switzerland. As he recalled the sad look on her face as they said good-bye, he decided that he must write a letter to her immediately. Never mind the problems at the factory for now. He looked for the writing paper.

An abrupt knocking on the door made him jump. "Come in!" he called. One of the workers put her head round the door.

"Please, sir." The girl could hardly look him in the eye. "We need to know how much to produce today."

"What do you mean?"

"It's Tuesday, sir. We always get the orders on Tuesday morning. Mr. Keen tells us exactly how much we need to make for the week."

Oscar scratched his head. Hadn't Tom mentioned something about an order book earlier? He wondered where it was kept. He pulled out the drawers, looked through the envelopes on the desk, but it was no good. The girl's expression grew more worried as she waited.

"You'll have to ask Tom . . ." Oscar said. "I mean, Mr. Harper."

"He normally gets the orders from the boss, sir—Mr. Keen, that is."

"Well, as you know Mr. Keen's unwell at present."

"Sorry sir, we know that. We were told you were in charge now."

"In that case," Oscar said, sounding more confident than he felt, "just find the order schedule for last Tuesday and produce the same amount."

"Yes, sir. Thank you, sir." She ran off gratefully.

Oscar spent the rest of the morning opening letters but he couldn't make sense at all of them. Out of his office window were some trees. He grabbed an envelope and began sketching. *Hmm, not bad,* he thought but he still needed to practice his shading if he was to improve. Never mind, when he was in Switzerland he'd be doing nothing but sketching and painting. Oh, to be out in the open, feeling as free as the birds in the sky. He hadn't meant to fall asleep but he must have nodded off. Tom Harper burst into the office and woke him up.

"What is going on, sir? Where are all the workers? They've gone home without completing the day's order."

Oscar realized then how quiet it had become. The machines had stopped and from the window he could no longer see the smoke coming from the factory chimneys.

"One of the girls came," Oscar explained. "She asked me what the order was for this week. I didn't know where you were, so I used my common sense and told her to do the same amount as last week."

"But it was the Easter holidays last week. All the shops were closed so our production schedule was for half the normal quantity. It's a disaster!" Tom's face had turned white with anger.

"It's not my fault," Oscar said. "How was I supposed to know? And anyway, where were you? Shouldn't you have been here?"

Tom's face turned red. "I . . . I had some urgent business to do in town for Mr. Keen, sir. I thought I told you about the order book. It's in this cupboard here." He went to the cupboard and took out a large notebook. Looking through it he said, "If we don't supply all the shops on our list then they'll look around for other manufacturers. This is just the opportunity that Seal's has been waiting for."

"In that case," Oscar said, "we must make sure our rivals don't hear about it. If we could get the order ready by tomorrow morning . . . "

"But how? The workers have all gone home."

"Just suppose we could, then would we be able to complete the order?"

"I suppose so," Tom said. "But we can't make them come back. They'll be eating their dinner by now."

Oscar went to the cupboard. "There must be some record of the employees. Their names, where they live, and so on. Ah, this is it," he said, lifting an enormous file.

"So?"

"So, let's go and round them up," Oscar said.

"What? You mean go to their homes and bring them back here?"

"Why not? We can start the ovens again, can't we?"

"Well, yes. But it'll mean working through the night and even then there's no guarantee we can complete the order by tomorrow morning."

"In that case," Oscar said, "the sooner we get started the better. Get the driver to come round and take us into town."

Chapter 5

A long night

The area where the workers lived was unfamiliar to Oscar. All the houses were built next to each other with no dividing wall. The sounds of babies and children crying, the smell of the city, was a far cry from his comfortable family home. Even his living accommodation in London, although small, had been clean and comfortable.

Tom knocked on one of the doors. A young girl opened it and her expression became serious when she saw both of them. "Go and get your father, child." The man came to the door, looking surprised.

"We need you back at the factory, Jones. Tonight," Tom said sharply.

"What? At this hour?" the man responded. "I've finished for the day. We completed the order like we were instructed."

"Come on, man," Tom said, "any fool knows that we didn't produce enough today."

Oscar saw that the man didn't like the way Tom spoke, so he stepped forward. "Look, we're in a bit of a mess here. It . . . it was my fault. I gave you all the wrong instructions. Now there's a chance—only a small chance—that we can meet our orders if we work a full night tonight. You're probably wondering what's in it for you? The answer is, I don't know. I can't promise anything in terms of extra pay. All I ask is that you do this for my father."

Tom was watching him closely with a surprised smile on his face. Oscar knew he had handled the man well and his words had had a positive effect.

"Alright then," the man said. "You'll want the other men, too."

"As many as possible."

"Oy!" the man shouted at his daughter. "Get yourself round to Billy, Fred, and Stanley right now and tell them to head for the factory." He turned to Oscar. "We have a system for rounding up the men. Fred, Billy, and Stan will tell their men and they will tell their men. But what about the women? We can't bring them out tonight. That wouldn't be respectable."

Oscar cursed under his breath. He hadn't thought of that. "Yes, we need the ladies to assemble the boxes and do the packing."

Tom spoke. "We may have enough boxes in storage. But we still need some women to do the packing."

"Look, I'll do it," Oscar said, suddenly. "Now come on—we haven't got a moment to lose."

By eight o'clock that night most of the men were there. A small number had refused to return to the factory again, but most of them were keen to show their support for the company.

Oscar rolled up his sleeves and helped to light the ovens. He took his turn preparing the huge vats of biscuit mixture under the guidance of the recipe maker.

It was hot and thirsty work and Oscar, who had not had the benefit of his supper, was weak from hunger. But he

couldn't afford to stop. By midnight the correct quantity of biscuits had been made, and the men slowly began to go home. At one point Oscar heard one of the workers say, "The boy did well tonight. Not as stuck-up as I expected."

He washed all the flour off his hands and face and began the next task: folding flat sheets of card into boxes. It was difficult work and he saw straight away that a change could be made to the design to enable the boxes to be assembled more easily. He would discuss it with Tom tomorrow.

At that moment Tom walked in. "We're winning—just about. The last lot of biscuits is going through the machine. It'll be at least three hours before they're cooled properly and ready for packing. The bakers have gone home. I told them they could clean their machines in the morning."

"Yes, of course, and tell them thank you. You should go home, too." Inside, Oscar's heart was sinking at the thought of being alone in the factory. It was getting cold and dark and at this rate he wouldn't be going home until the men were back for their early start.

"Before you go, Tom," began Oscar. "I'm grateful for your help today. I'd be even more grateful if you could avoid mentioning my mistake to my father."

"As you wish, sir." Tom bowed his head.

A group of three men came into the packing room. "What is it?" asked Tom. "I thought I said you could go home."

Oscar recognized one of the men. It was Jones, the man whose house they first went to. "We thought we'd give you a hand with the packing of the biscuits. Not that we have a lady's special touch or anything, but we want to help."

Oscar nodded gratefully, and his heart warmed. He'd been expecting a long and lonely night. Instead the men worked silently side by side and, after some initial mistakes, the men got a rhythm going without too many broken biscuits. By four o'clock the next morning all ten containers were filled with boxes. A loud cheer went around the group when Tom declared the production schedule was complete.

There was no point going home. The men found some blankets in the room where the workers took their breaks and then settled down on the floor. Oscar tried to go to sleep but although his body was exhausted—his back aching, his fingers sore from paper cuts—he felt a curious lifting of his spirits as he lay next to the men. They had all worked hard tonight. Yes, he'd made a stupid mistake, but he'd worked hard to fix it. Hopefully, there was no need for his father ever to find out.

"I was pretty foolish today, wasn't I?" Oscar whispered to Tom. "No, don't answer that. But I bet you're wondering," he continued, "how I could have made such a silly error."

"Well, sir . . ." Tom said, "I know your father sent you to London to learn all about the world of business and trading . . ."

"Tom, can I tell you something?" Oscar said. "I don't want to be a businessman. I've never wanted to be stuck in an office all my life. In fact, I'd rather be in prison!"

"A man has to earn a living," Tom said quietly.

"Oh, I know that, Tom. It's just that when I'm with my friends it's the only time I feel alive. We talk about the world, about how it should be run, about our feelings, and beautiful things, the stuff that really matters."

At that moment he was struck by how much he envied his friends in Switzerland. How they would laugh if they saw him now.

Tom's voice pulled him back to the present. "Forgive me if I'm speaking out of turn. But I was once like you. I had dreams of getting an education and seeing the world, all the things my father couldn't afford, but I had to start work at the age of fifteen. No choice."

"But you're so good at running the business," Oscar exclaimed. "You should have been put in charge of Keen's Biscuits instead of me." Tom looked at him. Oscar thought to himself, *actually, that's not a bad idea.* Yes, as soon as his father showed the first signs of recovery he would suggest to him that he give Tom the responsibility. And with Tom in place there would be no need for Oscar to stay any longer in Birmingham.

With that happy thought he fell asleep, exhausted.

Chapter 6

Oscar speaks to his father

Two weeks had passed since the near disaster at the factory when Oscar, Tom, and the rest of the men had been forced to work all night. The order was delivered successfully, and a few days later Oscar had some good news for the men. One of their London customers, Shannon's, had doubled their order of biscuits. It would mean working longer hours but the men were glad of the work. There was even the possibility of taking on some new employees.

Meanwhile Charles Keen was getting a little better. One morning Oscar found his father wide awake and trying to sit up in his bed.

"Help me, son, and for goodness sake get those curtains open. It's like a prison in here."

Oscar was surprised and delighted to hear his father complaining. He rushed to the side of his bed and lifted him up into a sitting position. He found extra cushions and settled his father back against them. When he drew back the heavy curtains the April sunshine streamed through the window.

"How are you, Father?"

"Feeling better. In fact I'm starving."

"I'm glad to hear that. You haven't eaten for a long time. What would you like?"

"Tell Cook to bring me a boiled egg and a piece of toast—no butter. Nothing too rich to start with. And a pot of tea. Much better than that stuff the doctor's been forcing down my throat." He pointed to the medicine bottle on his side table, which was half full of a dark brown liquid.

"So, my boy, how are things at the factory? Tom is supposed to report to me but he's not saying much, just telling me I should be resting and letting you and him get on with things."

"Well, Father, we've been very busy. Shannon's in London has doubled its order."

"Doubled, you said?" his father asked, nodding slowly with approval. "And any problems?"

Oscar had already decided not to mention the bad mistake he'd made. No harm had been done after all. Then he remembered his idea about Tom. Now was an ideal opportunity.

"Actually, Father, there is something I was going to say." Stupidly, he could feel his face reddening. "About Tom Harper, Father. He knows a lot about the company and is far better qualified than I to be running things while you're ill. He knows the factory inside out. He knows where everything is and how all the systems work. I was thinking . . ." he swallowed, "wouldn't it be better if you gave control of the decisions to Tom? Just until you're better," he added.

His father waited a while before responding. "Son, you have misjudged both yourself and me."

"I don't know what you mean."

"You know more than you think! You've been learning everything there is to know about business under

Mr. Allsop's expert guidance. That's why I sent you to London! Of course you're qualified!"

Oscar managed a weak smile. "You said I'd misjudged you, too?"

"That's because Keen's Biscuits is the family business. Call me proud, but I couldn't hand over control to anyone outside the family. Why, it would be unimaginable. When you have sons of your own you will understand."

Oscar didn't want his father to get upset so he said, "Yes, I see."

Charles reached to pull the bell behind his head, but Oscar said, "It's alright. I'll go down and tell Cook how hungry you are and ask her to bring you breakfast."

On the way down Oscar paused again at his father's picture. Here was Charles Keen, the proud owner of a successful company he'd worked hard to build. What a pity, Oscar reflected, that he'd been unable to persuade his father to let Tom take more responsibility. Thankfully, he hadn't mentioned it to Tom that night at the factory. No doubt Tom would have been very disappointed.

Chapter 7

Some shocking news

Oscar estimated that his father would be well enough to come back to the factory within a week. Each day he sat and took his breakfast with his father. They discussed the previous day's news and Charles outlined his plans for the company. It was a time to be optimistic.

Sometimes Oscar wondered if he should try again to argue Tom's case as a full-time replacement for him. But really that wouldn't be necessary as his father seemed to be recovering nicely. Oscar's thoughts turned back to Helena and his friends, William and Joel. He should write to them and let him know he might be able to join them soon, before the holiday ended. But Oscar found he never had a minute to sit down and write the letter. His days at the factory were busy and productive. Tom was doing a splendid job of making sure production continued according to demand, and they even began to have meetings about launching a brand new line of biscuits. Oscar had sketched some possible box designs, and he showed them to Tom.

"Only this time," Oscar said, "the plans must stay between us. We can't risk them falling into Seal's hands." Tom nodded.

A day later Oscar arrived at work to find Tom in his office, searching the cupboard. "Is everything alright?" Oscar asked.

"I'm afraid there's been another break-in," said Tom. "Those plans we made for the new line of biscuits have been stolen."

"Who's behind it? Is it Seal's again?" Oscar felt angry inside. How dare this company steal his ideas?

"In future, sir, why don't I keep all the confidential information at home?" Tom said. "No one will know."

"Good idea," replied Oscar.

But worse news was to come. The very next day he saw Tom at the factory absorbed in reading a newspaper. As Oscar came closer, he saw it was *The Daily Times*, a national newspaper read by the wealthy and most educated people up and down the whole of Britain. Tom's face was extremely red. "What is it, Tom? Are you alright?" Oscar asked.

"Nothing, sir," Tom said, shutting the newspaper quickly.

"Come on, Tom. I can see something is bothering you."

"Well, sir, I was hoping I wouldn't have to show you, but it's only a matter of time . . ."

Oscar's heart turned over as he was reminded of the day in Mr. Allsop's office when he received the bad news about his father. Tom clearly had disturbing news of some kind. "Give it here," he said, reaching out and taking the paper. "Where is it?"

"Page three."

Oscar found the page and began to read.

The newspaper story was about Keen's Biscuits. It began with a description of the company and how it had been established in 1870 by Charles Keen; it went on to list the biscuit brands that Keen's was famous for. Recently, the article said, the company had introduced a range of lemon cream biscuits that had become very popular. But then the emphasis of the article changed. The journalist had found evidence that Keen's Biscuits was using sugar imported from the Caribbean island of St. Christopher, where the workers in the sugar fields—called "plantations"—faced terrible working conditions. Long hours, poor pay, frequent beatings . . . The paper quoted the stories of some of the workers.

"So," the final passage ran, "as you sit down to have your afternoon tea and biscuits, spare a thought for those poor sugar workers and their unrewarded labor. You may find Keen's Biscuits do not taste quite so sweet after all."

Oscar went to stand by the window. Looking out at the trees, his first thought was, who will care? Perhaps it was wrong of him to think so, but what happened on a remote island thousands of miles away wasn't his or anybody else's concern. Then he remembered how Mr. Allsop, as part of his training, had taken him to visit the storage houses in London to inspect all the imported goods: sugar, tea, coffee. Together they had smelled and tasted supplies to test them for quality and freshness. He wondered why he'd never given any thought to where all these supplies had originally come from, or the conditions under which they were produced. But it was true. He had honestly never considered it before. Questions like that belonged to the business world; it was not what he was interested in.

But now a terrible feeling went through his body as words and phrases from the newspaper story came back to him: forced labor . . . horrible beatings . . . cruelty . . .

"Did you know about this, Tom? Is it true? How did the newspaper get the story? I must go and ask my father right now."

"No, wait!" Tom said. "We don't know if it's true or not. It might just be an attempt to ruin our good company name."

"If that's the case, then it's certainly worked. It makes me sick to my stomach to think about it, to think my own father might be a part of this. Imagine how the fine men and ladies of this country will react."

"My advice is to do nothing for now, sir . . . Mister Oscar." Tom said. "Challenging your father could be dangerous. On no account must you show him this newspaper. He is too ill for that."

Chapter 8

An argument

Oscar walked home from the factory instead of taking a train. Fine rain began to fall but he hardly noticed it. His thoughts and emotions were all mixed up as he marched through the woods on the family estate. Tom had said the newspaper story might not be true, but Oscar knew he was trying to be kind. Confused and disappointed, he had to face the truth. It was possible that the success of Keen's Biscuits was based on a horrible cruelty. How could his father have done this?

And to think he'd sacrificed his holiday and the chance to be with Helena—all for a struggling company whose good name had been damaged. He might have missed the chance forever to become close to her. A sudden picture of Helena came into his mind—her green eyes and fair curly hair—laughing with William on a snow-covered mountain in Switzerland.

Oscar increased his pace and soon arrived at the house. Frank, his father's servant, was coming down the path.

"Back early, sir? Your father's looking a lot better today. The doctor has seen him and has declared him fit for work in a few more days."

Really, thought Oscar, *you have no idea. In a few more days there might not even be a company.*

He ran up the stairs two at a time and pushed open the door to his father's room, no longer concerned about disturbing his invalid father.

Charles Keen was sitting up in bed, reading through some letters, and he was shocked by the sight of Oscar.

"Have you seen this?" Oscar threw the newspaper so it landed on his father's bed.

"What is it?" Charles reached for the paper and his eyes traveled over the page.

"Go to the third page. It's a wonderful bit of publicity for your company," Oscar said. His father didn't seem to notice the bitterness in his voice for he smiled and looked eagerly at the paper.

As Charles read on, the smile on his face faded. "What is this? This . . . this utter nonsense? What an evil accusation to make!"

"Why do you call it evil? Because it's not true? Or because it's speaking a truth that you've been trying to hide?"

"What do you mean?" his father asked.

Oscar sighed. "Is it true what the paper is saying? About our sugar supplier using forced labor?"

"Of course it isn't true. Well, we do get our supplies imported from St. Christopher, yes, but I've never heard . . ."

"So what you mean is you don't really know. It's *your* company, Father, and you don't even know what's going on!" Oscar gave a bitter laugh. "The magnificent Keen's Biscuits! I'm so proud to be a part of it now. So lucky that I will be able to take over your wonderful firm."

"How dare you be so ungrateful?" Charles Keen shouted. "Don't think I don't know you've been wasting your time in London, fooling about with those no-good friends of yours."

Oscar felt his stomach turn over and his heart begin to thump. Oh no, he thought. His father saw he had the advantage and continued, "I've been paying you a generous allowance. I arranged your training so you could learn the business, and what use has it been? I sent you to London as a trainee and I expected you to come back as a man. But you've been doing nothing but wasting time."

"But . . . how did you find out?" Oscar asked, a deep sense of shame spreading through him. Surely Tom hadn't told his father, not after his promise not to.

Charles Keen held up a sheet of notepaper. "I had this letter from Mr. Allsop this morning. He was inquiring about my health and wishing to apologize for failing in his duty of teaching you the basic principles of business. But it was difficult when you were often late for work, and when you *did* appear you were often too exhausted to concentrate on the job. He's apologizing to me for *your* failures! Can you imagine how that makes me feel?" Charles shook the letter angrily. "Mr. Allsop is a trusted friend of mine and you have let us both down." He continued, "I had decided not to say anything to you, to give you the chance to prove yourself, at least until you came in here shouting. Your mother would have been ashamed of . . ."

"But I didn't want to be part of this company anyway," Oscar cried. "You and Mr. Allsop took it for granted that I would want to take over the business one day. Not once did you ask me about *my* plans or how I wanted to spend my future." Here was his chance to tell the truth at last. "I'm sorry, Father, but I just don't care about business!" He loosened the tie around his neck and then threw it to the ground, while his father watched with a shocked expression. "All your life," Oscar continued, "you've worked hard for this company of yours and where has it got you? It's made you ill and now, with these damaging claims, Keen's Biscuits will never survive. The world has changed. There's more competition. I know all about the problem with Seal's and . . . Father, oh Father, what is it?"

Charles had fallen onto his side and his face had gone white. Oscar was too afraid to check if he was still breathing. He ran out of the room and shouted downstairs. "Quick! Get the doctor. My father's collapsed again."

The next hour was the longest in Oscar's life. If his father died, if he'd made him die, he would never forgive himself.

Eventually the doctor came out of the room, and Oscar rushed past him to be with his father. His face was still as pale as the white pillow he lay upon; all the pink color in his cheeks had gone again.

"Father?"

Charles Keen opened his eyes. Thank goodness he was still alive. "I'm sorry, Father. I never meant any of that. It was stupid of me. You're right. I know I let you down."

His father's voice was rough; it sounded almost unrecognizable to Oscar—like the voice of an old man. "No, perhaps you were right, my son. I'm too old for this game and I can see now that you really don't want to run Keen's Biscuits. You are young, with your own life to lead. Perhaps it *is* time to give up the company." He closed his eyes again and went to sleep.

A few hours later, when his father was well enough to speak, he said to Oscar, "Come here, son. I want you to arrange a meeting with the owner of Seal's and speak to my lawyer, too. We'll get an agreement drawn up. We can get a good price for the company and all our equipment." Oscar noted that the color had already returned to his father's cheeks.

"Will Seal's keep the factory open?" Oscar was thinking particularly of Tom and hoping that he could be promoted to a manager.

"I should think so if this Seal's has any sense. I have some good workers. But soon that won't be our concern." It seemed to Oscar that all the lines on his father's face had become smooth again. Charles could at last retire and enjoy the fruits of his labor.

Although he tried to concentrate on his father's instructions, an emotion had been growing inside Oscar that he tried to ignore. It was a feeling of utter relief. No more getting up early. No more long hours at the factory. Above all, no more responsibility. Yes, of course he felt sorry about leaving the factory workers. Lately they'd become like companions to him, but never mind. Soon he was going to be free again. His father had made absolutely the right decision. Even the weather seemed to support this fact. The depressing rain of the morning had given way to glorious late afternoon sunshine. Oscar felt like running into the garden and laughing. Soon he'd be with Helena again, and back in control of his life.

Chapter 9

A sleepless night and a decision

The grandfather clock struck midnight. Oscar was still seated at the desk in his room. It was time for bed, but he was too excited to sleep. He had just finished writing a letter: *Dear Helena, I shall be joining you in Switzerland in a matter of days. I just have a few loose ends to tie up and then I shall be with you for the rest of the holiday.*

He took out the card that she'd given him, which had the address of the boarding house on it. Oscar held it to his cheek and smelled the faintest traces of her rose perfume.

Oscar couldn't wait to see his friends again, William and Joel, as well as Helena. He had plenty of stories to tell them. How he'd make them laugh with all the tales from the factory!

He wrote the address carefully on the envelope, an act that reminded him of being in Mr. Allsop's office. No doubt he'd have to go back there after he returned from Switzerland. But wait! With no family business to run there was no need for him to complete his training under Mr. Allsop's supervision. Oscar laughed out loud. He could do whatever he wanted from now on. He could follow his dream of becoming a painter, instead of being imprisoned in a boring office. The candle was burning lower; he really must go to bed. He couldn't stop smiling as he stretched out his legs under the blankets and he gave a sigh of joy. He was sure he'd be asleep within a minute.

The clock struck one and then two o'clock and sleep still failed to come. Oscar couldn't understand it. He rubbed at his eyes and then got up. He pressed his face to the window and gazed out into the blackness. All he could hear was the strange crying sound of a fox in the nearby woods.

He had to admit he'd made a mess of his life so far, but now everything had all worked out for him the way he wanted. Why then was he so restless? He climbed back into bed, tried sleeping on his left side and then his right. He cursed at the clock when it struck three o'clock. It was impossible to sleep.

He began to think of his father's decision to give up the factory. Earlier on he'd been convinced that it was for the best—best for his father to be free of the stress and worry and best for Oscar, too, in that he was no longer forced into the family business. And yet . . . Keen's was the family business, he thought. His father had built it from nothing and had dreamed of his son taking over one day. Suddenly Oscar thought of his mother and her final words before she died, "Look after your father, Oscar."

Look after your father. Look after your father. Her words echoed inside his head, until he reached a sudden decision. He wasn't going to go to Switzerland just yet. He had something far more important to do first.

"Are you mad?" Charles shouted. "Don't you remember our discussion yesterday? I'm selling the company and that's final."

Oscar spooned sugar into his tea and waited a moment to stir it, letting his father's anger wash over him.

"I shall go into the town today and inquire at the travel company about when I can get the next boat to St. Christopher."

"Do you have any idea how long it will take? Weeks! This isn't one of your little adventures," Charles said.

Oscar replied carefully. "Someone—we don't know who, probably Seal's—has been trying to ruin your reputation. For all we know, they could have paid the journalist to write that newspaper story. The only way to find out what the situation is is to go to the island to investigate—and that's what I intend to do."

"Then I'm coming with you. It could be dangerous out there," his father said.

"No, Father." Oscar was firm. "You'd never survive the journey. Now I need Frank to help me start packing. I shall be away for a couple of months so I will need to take plenty of clothing. You can put Tom in charge at the factory."

Oscar stood up to leave the table. "Father, I'm going to do everything in my power to make sure the Keen name is restored. Then, if you decide to sell the company, so be it, but let me do this first . . . please."

Charles let out a big sigh. "Very well, my son. You have my blessing."

Three days later Oscar was on board a ship in the middle of the Atlantic Ocean heading for America. From there he would travel to the small island of St. Christopher. The voyage would take over seventeen days in total. The journey was far rougher than he expected, and he spent the first two days in the grip of a terrible sea sickness. By the end of the first week he was glad to emerge from his cabin and go up on deck. Oscar looked out into the distance. Land was nowhere to be seen, just a perfectly straight line between the blue sky and sea. The view helped to empty his mind of worry, bringing him a sense of calm.

A voice spoke to him, and interrupted his thoughts. "It's been rather a horrible voyage, hasn't it?" He turned and saw a middle-aged woman dressed in white, carrying a parasol to protect her from the sun. She was pretty and reminded him of his mother.

They passed a few minutes in conversation. When Oscar told her he was heading for St. Christopher, she said, "They call it the garden of the Caribbean, you know. There is great beauty on that island." *And also great ugliness,* Oscar thought, *if the newspaper story was true.* She recommended to him a hotel to stay, and he wrote the name down. "Keep away from the local people. You'll be safer that way."

Before he set off on his journey, Oscar had written a letter to the sugar plantation owner—a man called Mr. Gaston—in which he said he wanted to discuss the possibility of increasing the order of sugar supplies. It was better to keep Mr. Gaston off his guard so he would have no reason to suspect Oscar before his arrival.

At long last the ship anchored at St. Christopher. Smaller boats were ready to meet the passengers as they left the ship so that they could be rowed to shore. Excitement rose in Oscar's chest. He admired the beauty of the landscape, the steepness of the mountains. It was an entirely different world and he could almost forget the reason for coming here.

The first task was to find the hotel that the woman on the boat had recommended. He looked around. A young woman, clearly a native of the island, was walking past

with a basket on her arm. She seemed to be watching him and she looked friendly, so Oscar approached her saying, "Excuse me, do you know where I might find this hotel?" He showed her the name he had written on the paper. Then he added, "My name is Oscar Keen. I've come from England."

The woman looked surprised for a moment and then bowed her head in greeting. "How do you do, sir? My name is Cecile Johnson." He was unsure about whether to offer his hand at first. But she shook it and her skin, he noted, was soft. She looked at the name of the hotel on the paper and nodded. "You must be exhausted," she said.

Oscar laughed and rubbed his eyes. "Well yes, just a little." Then he explained he had an appointment the following morning with Mr. Gaston of the sugar plantation. "Do you know him?" he asked carefully.

"Know him? Of course, sir! Everyone on this island knows Mr. Gaston. Come, we shall take your luggage to the hotel and they will serve you a glass of iced tea. You look as if you need it." She called a carriage and a few minutes later they pulled up outside a luxurious hotel, the Carlton. As Cecile climbed out she said, "It was nice to meet you, sir. If you need to know the way to the plantation I can take you there tomorrow."

"Well, that's very kind of you . . . but it's far too much trouble," Oscar said.

"No trouble at all, sir," answered Cecile. "Will ten o'clock suit you?"

Chapter 10

Challenging Mr. Gaston

The next day Cecile arrived at the hotel to pick up Oscar, and together they set off on foot to the north side of the island for his meeting with Mr. Gaston. On the way she pointed out various landmarks: the large square with the courthouse nearby, the church that had been destroyed by fire the previous year and then, as they left the capital, she showed him the luxuriant green forests in the distance. The colors were brighter than anything he'd seen in England.

After they had walked for about twenty minutes, Cecile said, "It's not far now, sir."

"Do you work for Mr. Gaston?"

"Oh no, sir. But I know some of his workers."

"Really? What kind of a man is he?" Oscar asked, suddenly nervous about his meeting.

"Look over there, sir. You can see for yourself."

Oscar saw a large white man wearing a light-colored suit that was slightly too small for his size. He wiped his sweating face as he spoke to some of the plantation workers. Cecile leaned close to Oscar, whispering, "I must go now but I will see you later," and then she slipped away.

Mr. Gaston must have sensed Oscar's presence for he turned around and smiled in greeting. "Welcome, welcome, young fellow," he said as he approached, putting his arm around Oscar's shoulder. "You've come to discuss some business with me, I understand."

"Yes that's right. Umm, but . . . could I possibly have a look around the plantation first?"

"The plantation? Why, of course. Follow me." He led Oscar to the edge of a field where the tall thin, leafy plants grew. "We'll start with the cane fields. Cutting the sugar cane is physically hard work so I use only my healthiest workers." Oscar saw workers swinging large knives to cut down the plants. The workers looked cheerful enough, he thought. They wore white clothes and large hats to protect themselves against the heat of the sun. Mr. Gaston spoke, and in doing so he answered the question that Oscar had been about to ask. "They have breaks every hour where they can stop and collect a drink of water."

"What about punishment? Do you ever need to punish them—physically, I mean?"

"Of course not. What good would beating a man do? I need my workers to be in top physical condition."

Oscar was pleased. So far he had found no evidence of the cruel conditions that the newspaper had reported.

"Perhaps I could speak to some of the workers?" Oscar asked.

"By all means," said Mr. Gaston, glancing across the field. "Let me see. Henry, come here! You too, Arthur. And one of ladies? Elizabeth! Come over here all of you and speak to this fine gentleman from England. He has some questions to ask you." Mr. Gaston turned to go. "Excuse me, I have some work to do in my office. I'll come back in, say, a quarter of an hour?"

"Er, yes, yes," Oscar muttered. "Fifteen minutes will be adequate."

Oscar stood in front of the three workers. He looked at the woman, Elizabeth, first. She looked young—about twenty, perhaps—it was difficult to tell. She seemed shy and wouldn't meet his eye. Oscar glanced down at her arms. They were covered with a series of cuts and scratches.

One of the men laughed. "Don't worry about those, sir. We get scratched all the time when we're out in the fields chopping down the sugar cane." Elizabeth smiled, as if in agreement.

"I see. And how often do you have breaks?"

"Every hour, sir."

"Good, good," Oscar nodded. "And does Mr. Gaston ever hit you? You must tell me if there are any problems of that kind."

"No, sir. It is very pleasant to work here."

"Thank you. That is all," Oscar said, relieved. The two men and Elizabeth nodded and went back to the field. He met Mr. Gaston as he was coming out of his office.

"Is everything alright?" Mr. Gaston asked.

"Yes. Everything seems fine. I will see you in a day or so to discuss some, er, financial matters."

Oscar walked slowly away from the plantation. He needed to be on his own to try and assess the situation. So was the newspaper report false after all? There seemed to be no evidence of any cruelty at all.

To think he'd put up with weeks on that ship, all because he'd believed some foolish newspaper story intended to ruin Keen's Biscuits. He would make sure he took a full report with him back to England.

Then Cecile appeared, and they walked along the dry path together.

"How was your meeting, sir?" she asked.

He explained then why he'd really come to see Mr. Gaston; he told her all about the newspaper's accusations and how he'd felt driven to investigate.

"What a relief it turned out to be nonsense!" Oscar laughed. "I can go back and clear my father's name."

Cecile shook her head and smiled, but her expression was one of resignation rather than amusement.

"What is it?" he asked, curious.

"You really have no idea, do you, sir?"

"What do you mean?"

"That little . . . *performance* that Mr. Gaston put on for you. *'Oh welcome, welcome. Come and speak to my workers,'*" she said in a voice full of disgust.

"I don't understand."

"He knew you were coming! He's used to these investigations—he just covers up. I can see him now sitting in his chair having a good laugh at having fooled you."

"But the workers . . . why would they lie and protect Mr. Gaston?" he asked. "If the man really was treating them cruelly then surely this was an opportunity to let me know?"

Cecile looked at him, and clicked her tongue. "Don't you realize these workers depend entirely on him in order to survive? If the plantation closes then they will have no job. No job means no money to feed their families. He can do what he likes."

Oscar shook his head and remembered the warning from the Englishwoman on the boat. *Stay away from the local people.* "How do I know you're telling the truth?"

Cecile spoke more calmly now. "I'll prove it to you, sir. We'll go back there tonight and you'll see what conditions are really like on Gaston's plantation."

At the hotel Oscar ate supper and retired to his room where he lay on the bed, desperately wanting to fall asleep. A sharp knock on the door made him fully awake again. It was Cecile, dressed in a long cloak which covered her head. "Come on, sir," she said. "You're going to see how the plantation really operates."

Chapter 11

A nighttime visit

They passed through the fields in darkness. Oscar tripped twice, and after the second time, Cecile put her hand into his and pulled him along as if he was a child. A lamp swung in her hand so he could make out the path in front of them but little else.

"Where are we?" he whispered.

"Nearly at Gaston's plantation. Look, there's the processing plant." She pointed and he could just see a large wooden building with a light burning inside. "That's where they take the sugar from the cane once it's been harvested."

Oscar heard a scream and then a man shouting followed by another high-pitched scream. It was definitely a woman's cry. The terrible noise was coming from inside the building. Oscar's heart hammered in terror.

"Is that Gaston?" he asked.

"Probably not. He's too lazy and too clever to do his own beatings. He has his assistants for that." Cecile spoke in a steady but bitter voice.

Oscar took a step forward but he felt the grab of Cecile's hand holding him back. "What is it? I must go in and stop it."

"No, you mustn't! Please, not yet."

"But we can't stand by and let that awful punishment happen." He tried to close his ears to the awful sobbing he could hear.

"It's too late. The damage is done on this occasion. If you make trouble now you won't change that fact. You have to look at the whole picture."

At first the anger inside him was like a firework about to explode. But as the noise in the hut died into silence, he began to see the logic of Cecile's argument. Rushing in now would only make things worse, he realized. *But what should he do?*

He barely had time to organize his thoughts when suddenly the door flew open, and there in the opening stood Mr. Gaston. Cecile hurriedly bent down and he followed her example.

Gaston called out into the darkness, "Stop, whoever you are, and explain what you're doing on my land."

Oscar looked at Cecile in horror. He was frozen by fear. A gunshot rang out and shocked them both into action. "Quick, sir, run!" They ran away through the fields. Although she was small, Cecile ran faster than Oscar, but then she lost her balance and went crashing to the ground. He tripped over her fallen body. They lay still on the dusty path trying to control their breathing so they could listen for Gaston's approach. Oscar put his arm over Cecile to protect her, and she began weeping with fear. He held her tight. "It's alright," he whispered. "He's going back in the other direction. We're safe."

They eventually got to their feet and began the slow walk back to Oscar's hotel. "I've never been so frightened in my life!" Cecile said, laughing now. He thought how natural it had been to hold her when Gaston was pursuing them—he had protected her

instinctively. Should he mention it to Cecile now? Apologize, or even make a joke of it, perhaps? No, he decided, there was no need.

They reached the hotel and then Oscar said, "Wait, I'm not thinking. I should be walking you home."

"No, it's alright, sir. The danger's over now."

"Please. I insist."

She nodded and led him on a short walk to a row of small houses made of sheets of iron and pieces of wood.

"Not as fancy as your hotel, I'm afraid."

He stepped inside into a room with a bed and pictures on the wall and a bookcase. She told him she was studying to be a teacher one day. In the kitchen area she made a fire and prepared some tea. Refusing her offer of something to eat, he shook his head. "I couldn't." Not after the events he'd just witnessed. He sat on the mat and leaned his back against the bed.

"You know, I had started to convince myself that the newspaper story was wrong, that it had all been a big mistake, Cecile, a false rumor from a rival company."

"You didn't want it to be true. I understand that." She took a sip of tea. "I hope I haven't made you hate me for this. I was almost tempted to let you go back to England believing that it wasn't true."

"Yet you knew all along, didn't you? Is that why you were walking near the boat when I arrived? So that you could meet me and tell about . . . this?" He knew when he looked at her that it was true. "You could have just told me, Cecile. Was it really necessary to make me witness that tonight?"

Her face was unhappy as she heard the bitterness in his voice. "I had to let you see the situation for yourself," she said. "Perhaps that was wrong. Forgive me."

A mosquito landed on his sleeve and he shook it off.

"You know, there's something I've been wondering . . ." Oscar thought back to his initial conversation with Tom Harper about how his father Charles was losing his grip on the business, upsetting suppliers by trying to get sugar for a cheaper price. "Perhaps my father licensed Gaston as a new supplier without fully understanding what he was doing. In which case he is only guilty of ignorance."

Cecile shook her head. "I was here when your father cancelled the agreement with the original supplier. I saw it with my own eyes."

"What? My father came *here*? To St. Christopher? He never told me that." Oscar still couldn't believe his father was implicated. "You must be mistaken. Anyway, all I can do is to move back to the old supplier. Do you remember who that was?"

"He sold up when Keen's stopped accepting his sugar harvest. He couldn't make a profit with the lower prices that Gaston was prepared to accept."

"How do you know all this?" asked Oscar.

Cecile smiled. "I know because the supervisor of that plantation was my father. He tried really hard to represent the workers. That plantation had the best working conditions on the island. It broke his heart to see the plantation close and all those workers lose their jobs. Gaston took some of them on but he pays them almost nothing! Before my father died I promised I'd do something to help the other workers, but I was powerless until you came to the island."

Oscar was lost for words, thrown into confusion again. It had been a long difficult night. "Help me, Cecile. Tell me what to do now."

"I think you already know what you need to do. We have to confront Gaston!"

After tonight it was the last thing he wanted to do.

Chapter 12

Confronting Mr. Gaston

Oscar woke up in his hotel room the next morning to the sound of birdsong. Sunlight streamed through the window, making patterns on his bedsheet. His first thought was of Cecile, of the danger they had faced at the plantation last night and then their conversation afterwards. Between them, they had agreed that the only solution would be to talk to Gaston and to try to agree on better terms for the workers. It was a long shot, but what else was there to do? Switching to a new supplier, if they could even find one, would only cause more hardship for Gaston's workers.

As Oscar washed his face he reflected that this was exactly why he had never wanted to go into business in the first place. All the secrecy and double-dealing. His father and Seal's, the rival company, were each as bad as the other. If that's what being a businessman meant, then you could forget it!

"Don't worry. I know you're an honorable man." Oscar turned around to see Cecile at the door. "You were talking to yourself. You must be troubled." She spoke in a light and merry voice and he couldn't help but smile at the way she had begun to use his first name. He liked it. "Remember," she said, "we need to go and see Mr. Gaston this morning. I'll wait downstairs for you."

Five minutes later they walked in tense silence toward the plantation. Out of nowhere came the urge to hold her hand, as they had done last night. It was ridiculous. *You need to grow up and start acting like a man,* he told himself.

Mr. Gaston said, without greeting, "We had intruders last night. Luckily for them I didn't shoot them dead. Next time they may not be so lucky."

Oscar and Cecile glanced at each other. Did Gaston know it was them?

"Mr. Gaston," Oscar began, trying to imagine himself in his father's shoes. "We must speak about a very important matter." Mr. Gaston tipped his head to one side with an unpleasant look on his face.

Oscar continued, "You . . . I mean . . . you are not aware that I am now the new owner of Keen's Biscuits."

"What do you mean?" Mr. Gaston's eyes narrowed.

"My father has been ill lately and, to cut a long story short, he's transferred all decision-making powers to me."

Gaston gave a short laugh and then traced his stick on the ground silently.

"I want to make some changes to this plantation and the way you are running it."

"Now look here," Gaston cautioned. "You can't tell me how to run my plantation. What's your father doing putting a boy like you in charge? He must be ill. Ill in the head."

Oscar took a deep breath. "I have seen enough evidence to prove that the way you treat your workers is monstrous. Unless you make some changes, we'll find a new sugar supplier."

"Be my guest. You won't find cheaper prices for your sugar anywhere on this island. Your father knew that and so should you."

Oscar's mouth felt as dry as the dusty path they were standing on.

"So," Gaston went on, "answer this question. Are you prepared to pay more for your sugar? If you say yes, then perhaps I'll look at your terms."

"I can't promise that," Oscar said. "The answer is, I simply don't know. Show me the prices we've been paying you up to now."

Gaston stormed off into the office building and came back with a document dated the previous year. Oscar ran his eye over the pages remembering just enough from his training with Mr. Allsop to make sense of the figures. He looked at the two signatures, *Mr. Gaston* and *Charles Keen.* That was odd. It didn't look like his father's handwriting at all. Was his father ill at the time when he'd signed the contract?

"Mr. Gaston, how did my father seem to you when he was here?"

"Seem? In what way?" Mr. Gaston had noticed the change in Oscar's voice and spoke more gently himself.

"I mean, did he seem unwell in any way, or maybe confused?"

Gaston rubbed his chin while he thought. "No, no, not at all. He was in good health, not confused about anything. Now this contract is a valid document, young fellow, and I won't have you implying . . ."

"I'm not implying anything," Oscar said. "The situation is this. I'm going to keep you as a supplier but there are certain terms you must agree to. Cecile?"

She pulled out a list of demands that she'd helped him write out last night. Her knowledge was so much more considerable than his because her father had once had a senior role at a sugar plantation.

"What's this?" Gaston said, reading the paper. "My workers must have regular food and drink breaks? The women and men must be given proper clothes for their comfort and protection. The machines must be inspected twice a year, and all accidents to be written down in a report book. No physical punishment, and . . . wait a minute . . . a minimum wage for the workers?" Gaston held out the list for Oscar. "Forget it. I can't afford to do all this."

"Look," said Oscar, finally losing patience. "The fact is if I don't put this right, here and now, then Keen's will go out of business and you'll be in a worse position. Yes, you could look around for another company to supply to but that would mean starting from scratch. Better the devil you know, for both our sakes."

A long silence followed. Cecile said, "Of course we could always open the plantation where my father worked again. I'm sure Mr. Keen could help financially." She looked at Oscar and Oscar nodded. "I could run it and take your workers with me," she finished.

"You? Don't be stupid," Gaston said. "It's a man's job. You'd never do it."

Oscar said, "She would, with my help. Do you want to take the chance?"

"Alright, alright," Gaston said moodily. "I'll agree to those conditions but I want a guarantee from you that you will increase the amount you're prepared to pay per ton."

"It's a deal." Oscar held out his hand to Mr. Gaston. They shook hands.

On the way back from the plantation Oscar said: "That was brilliant when you threatened to run the other plantation. For a moment there I thought you were serious."

A solemn look came over her ordinarily cheerful face. "Perhaps I was."

Chapter 13

Time to relax

Down on the bay, Oscar watched a group of young boys play fighting and running races across the sand. An old man led a donkey with groceries on its back.

Cecile was at his side. They felt no need to speak. He removed his shoes and rolled up his trousers, delighting in the feel of the hot sand between his toes.

"Let's have a drink," Cecile said. "You go and sit on those rocks over there and I'll fetch us one." He watched her tiny figure as she walked away.

For the first time in his life his mind felt wonderfully clear—as clear as the blue sea nearby where little fish and turtles swam. He had never had that feeling before. It was exhilarating. Cecile came back with two glasses of thick orange-colored liquid.

"What's this?" he asked.

"Try it and see if you like it."

He sipped at the thick liquid. It had a sweet but distinctive taste, like perfume.

Cecile looked at his face. "Not sure yet, huh? It's juice from the mango, one of the fruits that grows here."

"I could get used to it," he said, smiling.

She held out her glass in the air. "Congratulations! You did it. You actually did it. You can draw up a new

agreement so that he can't break the law like he has been doing. Get it printed in that newspaper to show that Keen's has taken action."

Oscar still couldn't believe he'd managed to get Mr. Gaston to change his mind. He looked across at Cecile. Surely she wasn't crying. "Well? What is it?"

"It's nothing—and everything," she said and laughed. "I could sit here all day but I must get back to my studies now." She paused. "You did something very important today. You should be proud of yourself. You will make the workers' lives a lot easier." And then she was gone.

He sat and thought for a while about his father. He still felt very upset about the action his father Charles had taken in switching to Gaston's plantation. Even if his intention had been to reduce business costs, he should still have made sure that Gaston was behaving responsibly.

Cecile told him he'd scored a victory, but suddenly a coldness went through him and he trembled in spite of the steaming heat. He'd promised Gaston a price increase but hadn't specified exactly how much. He had no idea how much extra the company could afford to pay. And suppose Keen's Biscuits failed anyway in spite of his attempt to save the company?

He decided to go back to the hotel and write to Helena. It would be weeks before she received his letter, but he had to get his thoughts and feelings down while he was away from Cecile. He just seemed to get confused when he was with her.

Dear Helena, he wrote. *Forgive me for not writing sooner to you. I am sending this from the island of St. Christopher in the Caribbean, where I was forced to come and sort out some urgent business for my father. You would love the landscapes here. The sea and the sky are of the brightest blue, like nothing we have ever seen in England.* He paused and read through his note. Why on earth was he writing nonsense about the landscape? It was disturbing to realize he was having trouble picturing Helena in his mind—her pale skin, fair hair, and green eyes.

The mango juice had made him sleepy. But he couldn't settle when he tried to lie down on his bed. He felt irritated with himself, and restless. What he most wanted was to be talking with Cecile again about the business.

Dare he go and find her? Why not? He left the hotel. With every step he took his excitement grew. He willed himself not to run—he must stay calm and not alarm her with his feelings. Often when he looked at her she seemed to be assessing him, weighing up whether or not she could trust him. And then she'd laugh and her whole face would light up, and the amusement would remain in her eyes and on her lips for a long time afterwards.

In a few minutes Oscar was standing at the entrance to her house. *This is madness,* he told himself. *You'll be leaving soon, going back to England,* and yet . . . His desire to see her and spend time in her company was too strong.

At her door he hesitated, now afraid of knocking. He knew what would happen if she answered the door.

Chapter 14

A surprising visitor

Finally Oscar tapped on the door of Cecile's house. No reply came. He walked around to the fields at the back of the house, noticing the mango trees whose branches were weighted with ripening fruit.

What to do next? Should he lie down in the shade until she came back, or go to the plantation to check that Mr. Gaston was following the conditions properly? Once again he began to worry whether Keen's Biscuits could afford to increase the payment to Gaston.

He sat down under the tree and pulled a notebook and pencil out of his pocket and began doing some calculations. Some of his lessons from Mr. Allsop must have sunk in because he remembered how to calculate the exact amount needed to make the company profitable.

A shadow came over him and with it the warm flowery perfume of Cecile, which had already become deeply familiar to him. He turned around in delight.

"Thank goodness you're here," he said. "I've been waiting for you to come back. Just working out some figures to pass the time. Trying to see how to make the company stay profitable . . ."

"Why not ask your father's advice? I've just seen him getting off the ship."

"My father? But that's impossible. Are you sure?"

"I'm not mistaken. Remember I saw him when he came last time to the island."

"But how could he? He's far too ill to travel."

"I think he must have recovered. He looked perfectly well to me."

"Did you talk to him? What's he doing here?"

"I tried to. He walked like a man who was in a hurry. By the time I'd gone down to the port he'd disappeared. Perhaps he's heading for your hotel."

Oscar was surprised by this latest turn of events. Why had his father come to the island? Was it out of fatherly concern, or didn't he trust Oscar to sort out the mess he, Charles, had created? Was he ever going to be able to prove himself or would his father always doubt him? The joyous feeling from earlier had melted away to nothing, leaving a flat disappointment in its place.

He wanted time to think. Opening his notebook, he said to Cecile, "I really need to carry on working on these figures before I talk to my father."

"In that case, shall I go to the hotel and find him for you?" Cecile offered. "I'll tell him to rest and that you'll see him later."

"Yes," Oscar said. "And in the meantime I can make sure I haven't made any mistakes." He pointed to the calculations he'd already written down in his notebook.

"You look worried. What's happened to the confident businessman I saw earlier?" She touched his arm affectionately. "I'll go and find your father."

"How come you always know exactly what to do?"

"I do my best, sir." She bowed and ran off laughing merrily to herself.

Oscar didn't want to see his father until he worked out the figures. He found some shade under a tree where he made lists of different business forecasts for whether the sugar was priced at x amount per ton, or y or z amount. He would have to factor in shipping costs, too.

Soon he had a number of different pricing levels to show his father. Hopefully, he had done enough to impress him, to show him he hadn't completely wasted his training in London.

He was ready to find his father now. Although it had been wrong of Charles to deny using supplies from Gaston's plantation, Oscar thought he understood why. It was probably easier for his father to hide the truth from himself.

At the hotel there was no sign of Cecile or his father. He went to the reception desk. "Has my father arrived yet?"

"Mr. Keen? Let me check for you, sir."

Oscar watched as the clerk opened the large book that held the guests' details. Reading upside down, Oscar saw the last signature, *Charles Keen*.

"Wait a minute. Let me see that." He looked at the writing again. That wasn't his father's signature at all! He thought back to earlier on at the plantation when Gaston had shown him Charles Keen's signature on the contract. The one here was written the same as the one on the contract. But why? That didn't make sense. Unless, unless . . .

Just imagine, Oscar said to himself, *if an imposter—someone from Seal's, for example—has been pretending to be my father?* How easy it would be to come to the island and deliberately change sugar suppliers, just for the purpose of creating trouble later on for Keen's Biscuits. It was a completely mad thought, yet it also made perfect sense. He needed to speak to Cecile. Of course, she would have been fooled like everyone else was into thinking the man she had met before was Charles Keen.

The clerk spoke, "Are you alright, sir?"

"Have you seen a young woman, Cecile? My friend," he added.

"I have only just come on duty, sir."

"Then find me the person who was here earlier."

"Right away, sir."

Oscar's finger tapped the counter. A ball of tension was forming in his stomach. He didn't know why.

The clerk came back. "Your lady friend was here earlier. But she left the hotel with your father, Mr. Keen. Your father asked your friend if she would take him to see the mountains."

Chapter 15

Danger!

It felt to Oscar like he'd swallowed a stone that was rolling inside his chest. He walked away from the hotel clerks without saying anything. All his instincts told him something was wrong, but what?

He needed to think clearly and logically. Why would this imposter want to take Cecile up to the mountains? Last year, the man had fooled Cecile and Gaston into thinking he was Charles Keen, but he wouldn't be able to do it a second time—not now that Oscar was on the island. *This imposter, whoever he was, must be using Cecile to get me to the mountains,* he thought. And Cecile had innocently gone off with the man she thought was Charles Keen. How soon would she realize she'd walked straight into trouble? Oscar knew he must find them right away.

His mouth was dry and his heart thumped painfully against his chest.

He began to run in the direction of the mountains. His progress up the steep hill was slow, and the heat bore down on him like a great weight. There was a wood there, but despite the beauty and greenness of the landscape he could only think of danger.

"Cecile!" he called out, and renewed his efforts up the mountain. The branches of the trees tore against his clothing as he climbed higher and higher, his legs, although tired, refusing to give in. *If anything bad happens*

to Cecile I'll never forgive myself. I don't care what happens to me, I'll give up anything as long as she's alright.

And then he saw them both near the cliff top. It was definitely Cecile—she was wearing the white dress she had on earlier. With her was a short man with a hat. He could not see the man's face but he knew this was definitely not his father.

Now the man turned around and saw Oscar. The man grabbed Cecile firmly by the wrist, and she screamed and tried to pull herself free. They were dangerously close to the edge of the mountain top, and Oscar was terrified that she would fall crashing onto the rocks below. He ran toward them.

"Let her go!" Oscar shouted from a few feet away.

The man's face became clearer, and Oscar almost fell over when he saw who it was.

"Tom? Tom Harper?" he said, with a shake in his voice. "It's you. But what are you doing here?"

"Ha! There you are!" Tom shouted. "I thought she might bring you here!" Oscar was shocked by the roughness of his voice and the wild look in his eyes. He looked like a mad man, unrecognizable as Tom, the quiet foreman from the factory.

Cecile was now weeping in fear. Oscar brought his fingers to his lips. *Hush,* he mouthed, and she obeyed. He was moved by the look of trust in her eyes. She understood that she had helped him and now it was his turn to help her.

"Let her go," said Oscar again.

But Tom held on to Cecile. "Come and get her," he said.

Oscar's mind was racing. *Tom was the one with access to the design ideas for the lemon cream biscuits,* he thought. *Was it he who gave them to Seal's so they could copy Keen's?* None of it made sense, but Oscar knew he had to stay in control. Cecile's life depended on what he did next.

His mouth was dry and his voice shook, but he spoke quietly. "It was you then, Tom. It was you pretending to be my father—*you* who switched our sugar supplier. But why would you do all this, Tom? I don't understand it. I thought you loved my father."

"Him!" Tom laughed bitterly. "He betrayed me. If you want an honorable man then Mr. Keen is not your man."

"What did he do to you? Tell me," Oscar said, wondering how he could get to Cecile.

Tom was looking into the distance, still with his grip on Cecile, but lost in another world. "When I went to work for Keen's Biscuits seventeen years ago, your father was just starting out in business. He hadn't the first idea. He was useless. Worse than you! He didn't have the benefit of your London training. But who do you think it was who helped him to build the company to what it is now? Me!"

"But everyone knows how hard you work," Oscar said, forcing himself to sound calm. "I couldn't have done without your help when I arrived, and it's plain to see you did the same for my father all those years ago."

"Ha! And look what thanks I got for it! Your father promised me that one day I would be rewarded."

"And you thought that meant you would . . . what? Become a director?" Oscar saw from Tom's expression he'd guessed correctly. But why would Tom think that? Surely it was natural that Charles would eventually ask his only son to take over Keen's?

Tom said, "It was always me and him. We built Keen's up from nothing . . . together. Then one day, he had some wonderful news for me, he said."

"News?"

Tom went on, "Oh yes. The 'good news' was he'd arranged an apprenticeship for you in London and in two years' time you would be joining the company as a director along with him. Didn't I think it was splendid?"

Oscar moved closer toward Tom and Cecile. If he could keep Tom talking long enough he'd be able to reach her.

"Tom, I . . ."

Tom stared angrily at Oscar and almost shouted, "It was clear that there was no place for me! Your father was just using me. Good old Tom! Good enough to be foreman, but not good enough to be the real boss. Or even to have a share in the company! Like I said he's not an honorable man."

Oscar glanced at Cecile, seeing a look of panic in her eyes. Tom was drifting closer to the edge of the cliff. Both he and Cecile could fall over at any moment.

"So," Oscar said, quietly, again moving forward. "You decided to betray my father? You went to Seal's and offered to sell them all our company information? You did it out of spite. For revenge?"

"No! It wasn't like that. I met the men from Seal's by chance on board the ship coming here."

"When?"

"Last year. Your father, he was supposed to come but . . . he wasn't well enough, and I came in his place."

"So you got talking with the men from Seal's, and they told you they wanted to buy my father's factory? Is that right? Is that how it happened?" Oscar asked.

Tom nodded.

"And yet you knew my father didn't want to sell it." In Oscar's mind a picture formed of Tom and the men from the rival company coming up with a plan to make things so difficult for his father that he would be only too desperate to sell Keen's Biscuits. "I suppose they offered you a reward of some kind," he said.

"They said they'd make me a director if I helped them."

"By 'helped' you mean making as many problems as possible for us!" That's why Tom had switched sugar suppliers once he got to St. Christopher, knowing it would cause all that trouble later with the newspaper. And in the meantime Tom was also giving Seal's their precious design ideas!

Now Oscar was very close to Tom and Cecile. Unable to contain his anger any more, he ran at Tom. Tom suddenly pushed Cecile away and started to hit Oscar. He felt his head crash against the ground and he tasted blood inside his mouth.

"You're mad!" Oscar shouted. "Did you think you could get away with it? You'll go to prison for this!" He managed to get onto his hands and knees, but Tom had his hands around his neck.

"Stop it!" Cecile cried, trying to pull Tom away from Oscar. It was useless—Cecile wasn't strong enough.

"If only you'd stayed in London, none of this would have been necessary," Tom said. He reached into his pocket and pulled out a knife, holding it high just ready to drive downward. Oscar looked at the knife.

"But I wanted to help you . . ." Oscar began. And then he saw the knife plunging toward him; instinctively, he closed his eyes and lifted his arms to protect himself.

Suddenly Oscar heard a strange cry. He opened his eyes to see that his worst fears had come true. Cecile had run forward to try and stop Tom, and the knife had gone into her. Blood was spreading across her white dress and her skin had turned the color of ashes.

"Cecile! *Cecile!*" Oscar shouted. He held her close to him and began to cry himself. "Tom, help me please, for goodness sake." Tom stood still, arms at his side, as if he was in complete shock.

Then Oscar heard voices. He looked up and saw about five policemen, called by the people at the hotel, no doubt. They rushed at Tom and held him, then took him away. Two local people who had followed the police lifted Cecile carefully and told Oscar they were taking her down to the hospital at Basseterre, the island's capital.

One of the policemen helped Oscar to his feet. "Are you alright, sir?" he said, in concern.

"I'm fine." He wasn't worried about himself and his few cuts and bruises. His thoughts were all about Cecile. Suppose she died. He prayed to himself that she would be alright.

Chapter 16

A difficult decision

Two weeks later Oscar was packed and ready to leave St. Christopher to return to England. His sketchbook rested on top of his case. How absurd it was that its pages had remained completely blank. He'd spent a month in one of the most beautiful landscapes in the world, and even then hadn't been inspired to pick up a pencil and sketch. He was not a real artist. He had no great talent like William. He didn't even have the passion.

"Nearly ready, sir?" inquired the hotel clerk, as he came into the room. "We'll take your cases down to the port." Oscar tipped him and went out onto the balcony for the last time. He picked a red flower shaped like an umbrella and pressed it between the pages of the sketchbook. It had given him a new design idea to put on the packet of Keen's Cream Biscuits.

Oscar went into the reception area where Cecile was waiting for him. She still had difficulty standing up straight but otherwise she had made an excellent recovery so far. The wound that Tom Harper had caused had not been too deep.

Oscar had visited her every day in hospital, sitting by the side of her bed, sometimes holding hands, always talking. Then, when Cecile was able to walk a little, he had supported her while they went into the hospital garden and sat side by side on the bench. There was no confusion in his mind. He admitted to himself that Helena was now a distant memory. No longer could he picture her face or feel the emotion for her that he once had. She had faded into indifference.

"I wish you could come to England with me, Cecile."

"You know that's impossible. My life is here."

Oscar smiled sadly. "I know, but a man can dream, can't he?"

"Anyway, who else is going to keep an eye on Gaston and make sure he keeps to the agreement?"

Oscar's mind came back to the present.

"I'll come with you down to the port," Cecile said.

"Are you sure? We can say good-bye here if you want," he said, but inside he was glad she was coming.

Oscar also thought of Tom, who was still in the island's jail following his arrest and trial for injuring Cecile. Neither Oscar nor Cecile blamed Tom entirely for what had happened, but still Tom had tried to bring the company down—and murder Oscar. Oscar had given evidence at Tom's trial in court. He had five more months to serve of his prison sentence and then he would be released and sent back to England. Once there, Tom would probably be jailed again for his role in almost ruining Keen's Biscuits.

Oscar and Cecile walked side by side as they had done so many times, his pace exactly in time with hers. Their arms touched occasionally.

"Are you sure you're well enough?"

"Yes, I'm fine. Will you write to me?"

"Always. I promise. And maybe one day you'll come to England and I'll . . ."

"Maybe one day," she said.

The ship was in the harbor. The little rowing boats were ready to take the passengers to the ship.

"I've got something for you." Cecile put her hand inside her pocket and pressed a small box into his hand. "Go ahead, open it."

Inside the box was a small polished stone. "What is it?"

"It's a Tiger's eye. It belonged to my father. It's to bring you luck and happiness."

Cecile had already brought him happiness, but he would certainly need luck when he returned to England. Oscar had decided that he would encourage his father to retire and he would run the factory from now on. It wouldn't be easy. There was the company's good name to restore—never mind Seal's to deal with. He would be starting from the beginning but he was determined to keep Keen's Biscuits within the family. One day he would marry and have children and they would take over from him—*if* they wanted to. But that was a long time in the future and for now he was looking forward to seeing his father again. He felt without a doubt that Charles would be proud of him. Finally he had honored his promise to his mother.

Oscar gazed up the sunny sky, the brilliant blueness that was reflected in the sea. He closed his eyes and pictured the sandy beaches, the wild flowers on the hills, trying to commit them to memory. There was no need to do this with Cecile. Although they would be separated by distance, he had the feeling that he would carry her around within him forever.

The other passengers were already boarding the rowing boats. Oscar kissed Cecile on her cheek for the last time.

"Are you ready, sir?" the boatman said.

Oscar took a deep breath and let it out. *Yes, I am ready,* he thought. *Ready at last.* He climbed into the boat.

Review: Chapters 1–5

A. Match the characters in the story to their descriptions.

1. _____ Helena	**a.** Oscar's father
2. _____ Mr. Allsop	**b.** the foreman of the biscuit factory
3. _____ Tom Harper	**c.** an old friend of Oscar's father
4. _____ Charles Keen	**d.** one of Oscar's artist friends

B. Choose the best answer for each question.

1. Oscar's ambition is to _____ .

    a. be a successful businessman

    b. travel the world

    c. become a famous artist

    d. work for Mr. Allsop

2. Why must Oscar go to Birmingham?

    a. He has lost his job in London.

    b. His friends are staying there.

    c. His father is ill and needs his help.

    d. There is an important art exhibition.

3. Why does Oscar make a mistake at the factory?

    a. He couldn't find the order book.

    b. He was too busy sketching trees.

    c. He made the workers upset.

    d. The equipment broke down.

C. Read each statement and circle whether it is true (T) or false (F).

1. Mr. Allsop speaks to Oscar to complain about his work. T / F

2. At the train station Oscar asks Helen to marry him. T / F

3. Oscar's mother died when he was only seven years old. T / F

4. Oscar's mistake was to order fewer biscuits than he should have. T / F

5. The factory men are angry about working at night. T / F

6. The women help to pack the biscuits through the night. T / F

7. Oscar wants to put Tom in charge of the biscuit factory. T / F

D. Complete the summary using words from the box.

ingredients	rival	competition
designs	price	enthusiasm

Charles Keen is ill and has lost his **1.** _____ for running the biscuit factory. The **2.** _____ of sugar and other raw **3.** _____ has gone up. Furthermore, his business is facing increased **4.** _____ from other businesses, including a **5.** _____ company called Seal's. According to Tom Harper, Seal's has been copying Keen's packet **6.** _____ .

Review: Chapters 6–11

A. Complete the crossword puzzle using the clues below.

Across

2. Keen's Biscuits imports _____ from the island of St. Christopher.

3. Oscar wishes he was in Switzerland with Helena, Joel, and _____ .

6. Cecile is a _____ of the Caribbean island.

8. Mr. Gaston invites Oscar to talk to his _____ .

9. There is more work in the factory because a customer _____ their order of biscuits.

10. At first, Oscar has a feeling of _____ when his father says he will sell the company.

Down

1. Charles does not want to give control to Tom because Keen's is a _____ business.

4. Oscar remembers his _____ telling him to look after his father.

5. A report in a _____ called *The Daily Times* criticizes Keen's Biscuits.

7. Working conditions on the plantations are said to be very _____ .

B. Circle the correct word or phrase in italics to complete each sentence.

1. Charles is *proud of / disappointed with* Oscar's work for Mr. Allsop.

2. Charles decides to *sell / close* the factory.

3. Oscar goes to *Switzerland / St. Christopher* by boat.

4. The woman on the boat reminds Oscar of *Helena / his mother.*

5. Cecile says that Mr. Gaston is *well known / unknown* on the island.

C. Choose the best answer for each question.

1. Why is Oscar glad after his first visit to the sugar plantation?

   a. He makes friends with Mr. Gaston.

   b. There is no sign of any cruelty to the workers.

   c. He has time to explore the island with Cecile.

   d. The workers have told him the truth.

2. What does Mr. Gaston do when Oscar and Cecile return to the plantation at night?

   a. He fires a gun into the air.

   b. He sets a dog on them.

   c. He chases and catches them.

   d. He calls the police.

3. Why does Cecile care about the conditions for the plantation workers?

   a. She wants to work at the plantation one day.

   b. She is doing research for a newspaper story.

   c. She has relatives who work on the plantation.

   d. She made a promise to her father to help the workers.

Review: Chapters 12–16

A. Number the events in the order they happened (1–10).

_____ Oscar tries to write a letter to Helena.

_____ Oscar accepts a gift from Cecile.

_____ Cecile is accidentally stabbed by Tom.

_____ Oscar runs up towards the mountain.

_____ Oscar and Cecile have a drink on the bay.

_____ Oscar learns why Tom hates Charles.

_____ Oscar finishes the business report for his father.

_____ Cecile tells Oscar his father has just got off the boat.

_____ Oscar makes a new agreement with Mr. Gaston.

_____ The hotel clerk tells Oscar that Cecile has gone to the mountains.

B. Read each statement and circle whether it is true (T) or false (F).

1. Oscar is nervous about going back to the plantation to see Mr. Gaston.   T / F

2. Cecile's father once worked for Mr. Gaston.   T / F

3. Oscar is puzzled by his attraction towards Cecile.   T / F

4. Tom takes Cecile to the mountains so that Oscar will follow.   T / F

5. Tom tries to kill himself.   T / F

C. Choose the best answer for each question.

1. Why does Gaston initially refuse to agree to the new working conditions?
   a. He thinks he cannot afford it.
   b. He enjoys being cruel.
   c. He does not like Cecile.
   d. He only wants to deal with Oscar's father.

2. On the island Oscar's romantic feelings toward Helena _____ .
   a. increase
   b. stay the same
   c. weaken
   d. turn to dislike

3. Why is Oscar keen to finish his calculations?
   a. So he can relax with Cecile.
   b. He wants to give them to Mr. Gaston.
   c. He is no good with figures.
   d. He wants to prove to his father he can do business.

4. Tom expected Charles Keen would reward him by _____ .
   a. sending him to London on a training course
   b. helping him set up his own business
   c. making him a director of the company
   d. giving him a lot of money

5. In the end, Oscar realizes that he should _____ .
   a. stay on the island with Cecile
   b. run the biscuit factory
   c. marry Helena and have children
   d. become an artist

Answer Key

Chapters 1–5

A:
1. d; **2.** c; **3.** b; **4.** a

B:
1. c; **2.** c; **3.** a

C:
1. F; **2.** F; **3.** T; **4.** T; **5.** F; **6.** F; **7.** T

D:
1. enthusiasm; **2.** price; **3.** ingredients; **4.** competition; **5.** rival; **6.** designs

Chapters 6–11

A:
Across:
2. sugar; **3.** William; **6.** native; **8.** workers; **9.** doubled; **10.** relief

Down:
1. family; **4.** mother; **5.** newspaper; **7.** cruel

B:
1. disappointed with; **2.** sell; **3.** St. Christopher; **4.** his mother;
5. well-known

C:
1. b; **2.** a; **3.** d

Chapters 12–16

A:
3, 10, 9, 7, 2, 8, 5, 4, 1, 6

B:
1. T; **2.** F; **3.** T; **4.** T; **5.** F

C:
1. a; **2.** c; **3.** d; **4.** c; **5.** b

Background Reading:

Spotlight on ... *Biscuits and biscuit makers*

Nowadays, biscuits come in all shapes and sizes.

The word *biscuit* is made up of two Latin words: *bis* (twice) and *coquere* (to cook). Biscuit literally means "cooked twice," because this is how biscuits were originally made — they were baked first and then dried slowly in an oven. Early biscuits were hard, dry, and not at all sweet in taste.

Famous British Biscuit Makers

Many famous biscuit makers began in the 1800s and they gradually introduced "fancy" biscuits to the British population. Huntley & Palmers and Fox's Biscuits are just two of the best-known companies. These companies began as small family-run shops or bakeries before expanding into large factories. It was customary for sons to take over the business when their fathers retired.

Companies were keen to test new recipes and develop new products. Popular biscuits included the Ginger biscuit, the Digestive biscuit, and the Custard Cream. The design of the packets and tins (the "packaging") was usually very colorful to attract customers.

Why Biscuits Became Popular

In the 19th century, there was a change in eating habits amongst the wealthy. Instead of a large breakfast and an early dinner, it became usual to eat a smaller breakfast, a hot lunch, and a late dinner. A tradition of taking "afternoon tea" began, with biscuits and cakes being served along with a pot of tea.

Did You Know?

As people in Britain began to travel long distances by train, the biscuit made an ideal snack for their journey. Huntley & Palmers gave away a free packet of biscuits to every customer traveling first-class from Paddington railway station via Reading, where their factory was based!

Think About It

1. Biscuits made today are far sweeter than early biscuits. Do you think that this a health risk?
2. How far does advertising and packaging work in encouraging us to buy biscuits?
3. What are some positive and negative aspects of taking over a family business?

Spotlight on ... *Sugarcane*

Sugar is one of the most popular foods across the world, but where does it come from?

Sugar is produced from the sugarcane plant — a tall grass with a thick stem. It is the stem of the plant that is processed to make the sugar.

Stages of Sugar Production

1. Sugarcane is planted in large fields, known as plantations.
2. At harvest time, the sugarcane stem is cut down by workers using a large knife called a machete. In some countries, machines are used.
3. The sugarcane stems are then taken to a mill, where the juice of the sugarcane is extracted (squeezed out).
4. The juice is boiled until it becomes a thick liquid called syrup.
5. The syrup is boiled further until sugar crystals begin to form.
6. Raw (unrefined) sugar is brown; to make white (refined) sugar, the raw sugar has to go through another process.

Top sugar-producers in 2011

No.	Country
1	Brazil
2	India
3	China
4	Mexico
5	Thailand
6	Pakistan
7	Colombia
8	Australia
9	Indonesia
10	USA

Source: United Nations Food and Agriculture Organization, FAOStat

The Growth of the Sugar Industry

Sugarcane grows best in a tropical climate. It was originally a native plant of Southeast Asia and was brought to the Caribbean Islands (then owned by the British and French) in the middle of the 17th century.

For the next two hundred years, over 10 million African people were removed by force and taken to work on the sugar plantations of Brazil and the Caribbean. Although this practice became illegal in 1834, the working conditions on the sugar plantations remained very poor and life was difficult for the sugar workers.

Think About It

1. How much should food companies care about how sugar is produced?
2. How important is it to buy products that are made under fair and proper working conditions?
3. If you knew that a company treated its workers unfairly, would you still continue to buy their products?

Glossary

apprenticeship	(*n.*)	time spent working for someone in order to learn a trade
carriage	(*n.*)	a vehicle with wheels, pulled by a horse, used for carrying people
commodities	(*n.*)	products that are traded
foreman	(*n.*)	a person in charge of a factory
imposter	(*n.*)	someone who is pretending to be someone else
landmark	(*n.*)	a place that is easily recognizable and used as a guide
mango	(*n.*)	a type of sweet tropical fruit
plantation	(*n.*)	a large tropical farm
servant	(*n.*)	a person employed to serve
sketchbook	(*n.*)	a book used for drawing
stuck-up	(*adj.*)	snobbish, believing that you are better than other people
sugarcane	(*n.*)	a tall grass used to make sugar
supervisor	(*n.*)	person who oversees work done by others
ton	(*n.*)	a unit of weight
vat	(*n.*)	a large container